Seeing Humming Tiger Lost Poems

By
AKIIES UGEREADT

Copyright © 2024 **Chaston Marshall Books**

All rights reserved. No part of this publication may be reproduced, distributed, or transmitted in any form or by any means, including photocopying, recording, or other electronic or mechanical methods, without the prior written permission of the publisher, except in the case of brief quotations embodied in critical reviews and certain other noncommercial uses permitted by copyright law. For permission requests, write to the publisher, addressed "Attention: Book Rights and Permission," at the address below.

Published in the United States of America

ISBN 978-1-962569-85-9 (SC)
ISBN 978-1-962569-83-5 (HC)
ISBN 978-1-962569-84-2 (Ebook)

Chaston Marshall Books
222 West 6th Street
Suite 400, San Pedro, CA, 90731
chaston.marshall@yahoo.com

Order Information and Rights Permission:

Quantity sales. Special discounts might be available on quantity purchases by corporations, associations, and others. For details, contact the publisher at the address above.

For Book Rights Adaptation and other Rights Permission. Call us at toll-free 1-888-945-8513 or send us an email at admin@stellarliterary.com.

Table of Contents

Out of the Swamp 1

Snack Time at the Bakery 2

We First Thought 3

Blessed Are They 4

Me While Listening to Kelis "Caught Out There" 5

My Eyes See 6

Dear Mind 7

The Ocean is Sad to Receive You 8

The Keys 9

Soaked In a Weird Color 10

Chaff Driven by The Wind 11

Age of Chaff 12

Carry Your Snoring 13

Somersaults In My Juice 14

My Art's Ambition 15

An End Never Came to Summer 16

North Pole 17

Kaput 18

Pain Free 19

Antidote 20

Seeing the Eyes of Me 21

My Flight Got Canceled 22

Just Know That… 23

Mine, Airplane 24

A Couple of Apples 25

Forgive Me My Brothers and Sisters 26
Revolutionary Wall Protects Me
(A Conversation with God) 27
Before You Started… 28
Prom 29
My Nephew 30
If You Should See 31
Deadlock 32
Stay 33
Impromptu 34
World 35
Enshrine 36
Taking the Reigns 37
My Nephew Rose into a Silk moth (Part 1) 38
My Nephew Rose into a Silk moth (Part 2) 39
Need for Sugar 40
Spoiled Tasting Rain 41
Magical Wall 42
Tiger Monsoon 43
Chewing On Rocks 44
The Breathless Tiger 45
Goodbye 46
Juice through your Hands 47
Wisdom as I 48
Masterpieces 49
Calculations 50

Out of the Swamp

A soul the heavens loaned us,
diamonds bequeathed in his name,
like microscopic gems in
the dirt flooding and glowing

A soul amazing and just
ignoring me just not to
be used or obtained, he creates,
gold to fill up captain's bright,

Trumpets, souls stone in their jeans,
pockets, connecting to the
ocean, in and out, ready
to dissect everyday lives.

Snack Time at the Bakery

Brown shrinking sweets heating good,
        things I eat recharges me and designs,

my business. Be sure to thank me for the
        finger work, all the jobs are fast,

mopping quiet dread, crumbs I left on stove,
        in your bowl, It's the least I can do for you.

Chewing brownies like gum, the Queen's job,
        and hurling language to move a body,

Screaming from the Queen, a boy is scuffing her,
        floors, her life, her time and her very existence,

I still have not faced the Queen, memories.

We First Thought

We're just hangin' out,
we're just shooting the breeze,
we're just getting a feeling on one,
another. In our orbit, this
grim feeling sails straight
through our aquarium.
You can close your eyes,
as the invisible tattoo points
to the fact that we don't love
each other as much as we
first thought. As we post
towards shore, we say to
ourselves. "We will never do
that again, this one has
revealed itself. Eventually
everyone gets to submit their,
judgment cards. Even though
we both were mostly eyes,
in a way that only worked
against us. We were never,
sure, of this other world
inside my head.

Blessed Are They

Blessed are they that turn around in lion caves,

Blessed are they that ride motor bikes in the bike lane,

Blessed are they that know deep within them, they are safe,

Blessed are they that call to their inner self for strength,

Blessed are they that sing songs to uplift their people,

Blessed are they that occupy good morals and use wisdom,

Blessed are they that march on the hills of progress,

Blessed are they that concern themselves with justice,

Blessed are they that follow the laws and change laws ill.

Blessed are they that swim with the oranges and catch dolphins.

Blessed are they that keep cloudy secrets and share no gossip.

Me While Listening to Kelis "Caught Out There"

I contemplate on not the fact that you're a liar
but instead, the notion that you lie to me. I am
your biggest supporter and I am to you but a
golden bug, something that deserves no voice,
no position, no life except to offer golden assets
and funds. You estimate me as a golden bug and
yes, I am indeed golden, but I am no bug. That's
right, I am no bug at all, what I am is a Tiger,
lurking, my halls (not yours). I am contemplating
the day when you have reached for the last
dime of mine and I have sent you ablaze out
onto the ocean.

My Eyes See

My eyes see upbeat spaces,
wind over water traces,
land singing alive and dumps,
places where you found, trumps,
words bound in a ground,
experiences for a good time around,
people willing to spend a dime,
on their boots filled with grime.

My eyes see deep sentences,
fire over water traces,
land jogging alive and stumps,
minds not prepared for these rumps,
days bound in a ground,
experiences that will sound,
people planning to drill,
with their boots by a mill.

Dear Mind

Dear mind, come back to me,
oh, too hungry mind, exploring,
the ethers and what not, I know,
that you have a short span but
I am usually trying to do something,
whenever you decide that it's time
to drift. Dear mind, I need you to
be diligent, steadfast and ready.
I will no longer allow you to float,
on in at any old time that you see
fit. I will demand the sharpness,
of a perfect orchard beneath the
claws of a bear. I will see to it,
that you are the striking,
illuminated key.

The Ocean is Sad to Receive You

The Ocean cannot maintain your high maintenance Persona. The Ocean is too busy serving everyone and Everything, a much noble calling compared to your meager crumbs, arguments, abuse, fights and impulses to lie to the police. I offer you to the Ocean and in, it's time to rejuvenate your soul. I offer you and my previous stone-like prayers to float somewhere safe while accepting that the Ocean may just be sad to receive you.

The Keys

What key the moon shall prove?
The key beyond your first glance?
It's in my hands, or sitting on an
infinite staircase meaning success.
As success is meant to clothe me
and my home. So, if I want success,
I will begin with a smile, extra light,
in my mind self-supporting, climbing,
higher each, and every day. What,
measure of anything unless it is,
success and a smile. My life is grand,
will continue to be grand, will look,
back and say, "boy was I grand",
keys, I knew, made the difference,
keys, I still hold exemplary.

Soaked In a Weird Color

There is love for this boundless thing.
A peach, a colored bird spoken to
In the morning. Sweet juice, sweet
voice clumsy beside my neighborhood.
I knew that skies were the limit but
in my city, in my household there was
only peace concerning aspirations.
The windows looked like clear glass
cement with a slight smell of old paint.
I sensed the dusty Tupperware, plastic
pitcher, instant microwaveable foods.
Yes, I was in a small room in the
kitchen, drinking something cold and
pink.

Chaff Driven by The Wind

I am flowing unconditionally,
red, hot tempered
categorically, awaiting your
tornadoes, eager to see your
hurricanes. I am unpredictable,
on your table, I once a steward
on your ward. I release my gas,
in the middle of your speeches.
I welcome more of those,
thrown tomatoes to adorn,
my clothes. I'll move as you,
listen.

Age of Chaff

This is the new burn,
it is speckled with age,
It is, me lighting my way,
through the darkness,
swimming with the dolphins
and the sharks, repelling the
sharks, laughing with the
dolphins. It is, me breathing,
sighing in relief that the age
of chaff was never me.

Carry Your Snoring

Carry your snoring and your heavy sleep with you.
If you should go to the market, be sure to get one,
for it. The weather won't forever be this clear to
shine. My landlord might remember to wake up,
just to hound you after all he is your landlord too.
Carry light your backpack must not weigh you down,
get enough water to put in that bottle, be careful,
with your food intake you don't want to overexert
yourself. Remember that you are in good hands,
yes, these hands helped raise you, helped teach you,
helped prepare you, conspired with God's hands to
keep you. Today, I am letting you go and watching,
you, travel off to heard, your own cows. I can't keep,
you to myself any longer, blessings.

Somersaults In My Juice

My friend Emilia was mischievous and always had
a plan boiling in her pots. She would do arts and crafts
at her house in the summertime. She had juice, freeze
pops and carbonated soda stored away for friends. I
believe she suspected that there were somersaults in my,
juice and she had a need to prove it. She tried to trick me with
her green magical face paint. It was some sort of
red lipstick that appeared green but once on the skin
mysteriously turned red. Once she smeared it on my lips,
I could tell by looking in the mirror that I was fooled, it was
ruby red and I was a closeted pre-teen. Luckily no one saw
me as I ran home to wash it off.

My Art's Ambition

Centipede, bold, my art's ambition, painted ink to own
the page, the canvas; essence.
Centipede, blown by brown ink speed and focus, my own art
the page, the canvas; essence.
Centipede, gold in your mind and painted ink to own
jazz a kissed canvas, music.
Centipede, rose alive dancing and focus to own
jazz a kissed night of music.
Centipede has something to prove.

An End Never Came to Summer

An end never came to summer, she would,
talk then pause, then pick right up again,
after months had passed. Her hair had red,
leaves at the end and beginning of her,
shoulders. She laughed with bees and little,
insects scurrying about. I cared not for Summer,
though, I really preferred Autumn, he was more,
my speed and crisp in my mind.

North Pole

I never told you that you are as cold as Antarctica,
and at the same time lovingly warm as Africa.
I never told you that when you're mad, I get scared.
I am 40 years old, and your anger still penetrates,
my soul.
I never told you that I love you without expecting,
To hear it said back.
I never told you that as I grow, I realize that our,
lives are not as in sync, as I first thought.
I never told you that you are probably my first love,
in human form.
I have told you that you can be chaotic.
I have told you that you are sophisticated.
I have told you that the sky repeats your beauty.
I have told you that I love you in the sincerest,
way.

Kaput

An eleven-minute egg, just yellow enough
on the inside to cream an egg salad, I know
because this is not my first tango.

I open the windows in my kitchen without
Struggle. Today I know my eggs will heat
the bowl calling for your mouth.

Seemingly large and within a couple of
Days, kaput.

Pain Free

House, boat weary on the water
now shifting my head while the
soul, relaxes, does not hurt.
House collecting bubbles, water
watery glare, out the window
now rocking so calm pain free.

Antidote

Upon the sickening winter
full of sugar white
quiet on top of thoughts,
icicles near and melted
with a hope that this antidote
will remove winter.
Upon the ripening spring,
healthy blood sugar
time to set sail on my own.

Seeing the Eyes of Me

I emerge inertia ever transforming
to succeeder seeing the eyes of me.

I tenderly anytime and naturally
looking for glory, defining purpose,

I emerge inertia ever transforming
the rain as it grounds itself on my face.

I hesitate to decide what these pupils
dark on the grounds are saying.

I emerge inertia ever transforming
the rain looking for glory.

My Flight Got Canceled

Excuse me. I am in a hurry,
I've got to get to the other end.

I won teacher of the year and
I am pressed for time, hope you
don't mind.

My previous flight got canceled
and I don't want to miss this next
one.

Excuse me. My flight got canceled
Can you please sit by the window,
I was drinking a lot at the bar.

These are my only pair of bottoms
And I don't want to piss these.
Thank you.

Just Know That...

Just know that our kids are smarter
than you give them credit for.
You don't have to water-down their,
Education and if you must be
super involved, do so with class and
a calm head. No need to run down to
the school with your hair on fire.
Just rather calmly ask the teacher
what it is the child is being taught and
how that will help them grow into
an informed adult.

Just know that our kids can
process diverse topics and rarely
need their parent's confirmation.
If you are worried about not being
able to answer a child's question,
then maybe you should research
and take your research from
varied sources so that you are
prepared.

Mine, Airplane

No laughs of happiness.
I spent almost $700.00 on a ticket
And I don't know when I am
going empty, I don't know when I
am going home. No laughs,
My flight attendant has an
attitude because I am leaning
back and apparently, that is against
policy. No laughs, no longer feeling
comfortable, realizing that others
may not see the title golden that
is dripping from my forehead.
As I get my apartment tour I am
sure, that I get no preferential
treatment, no laughs I am
still on that plane.

A Couple of Apples

So, you stooped to message me
right out of the trees and here
we are normal rolling in
sunset, stronger, sweet-voiced and
set on the people of this
land who come bursting in to
taste us with their stomachs on
fire, ablaze, desires
on like cigars, fired lamps just
the average day calmly.

Just me and Ben waiting now
for Justin and Sabrina
to catch the muscular wind
or the breezy meteors
or hands that slice us up good,
just me and dear Ben I cry.

Forgive Me My Brothers and Sisters

Forgive me for calling you Native yes and or Native American.

This was not meant to be an insult but rather simply what I was taught.

Forgive the immigrants, the migrants that wave racism as their breath and flag.

Their monuments will soon crumble as they are not a representation of you.

Forgive the Americans that maneuver out of your language for your people.

We can only imagine how hard it is to maintain your complete heritage.

Forgive our religions that overshadow the sanctity of pre-America spiritualism.

Forgive me my indigenous brothers and sisters for labeling you Native American.

Forgive me my Black Americans for failing to change your label after the 90s.

We are not a fan of these labels like Black American and African American.

Forgive these awkward politicians and their twisted laws that have kept us back.

Forgive our police force for their blemishes, a reflection of a lamentable small portion.

Forgive the responsible for Asian hate.

Forgive the responsible for Middle Eastern targeting and hate.

Forgive the ones that target any citizen of any Country.

Forgive us.

Revolutionary Wall Protects Me
(A Conversation with God)

The highway is so loud by my window.
> A window that protects me from intense engines.

Day to day, I must listen to blaring roads or cars.
> The white wall of my home is revolutionary.

The cars like to roam.
> The window is like the prayers of my parents, all oiled up.

Cars like to speed.
> The wall is like the hand of the Cosmos or God.

Fresh of speed.
> The white flower in my car falls to the ground singing.

> Oh, revolutionary wall why doesn't you protect me too?

> And God says, "You are simply not within reach."

Dear God, I pray to you too.
  God: "Yes, but you have a way of ignoring my signs and very glory perhaps you should be more confident and specific with your prayers, surrender them, don't worry and stay optimistic, that's called faith, not everyone is good at it, but it works just with the virtue patience, if you work at it, you can past the test. You will not get what you want by simply speaking words, you must put action into it and sometimes action must be plural."

Before You Started...

Before you started there was X-Men, He-Man, She-Ra, Chip n' Dale, Duck Tales, Jem,

    Thunder Cats, G I Joe, Smurfs, Inspector Gadget, Pink

    Panther, Teenage Mutant Ninja Turtles, Ghost Busters,

    Transformers and more.

Before you started there was people with likes, dislikes, jobs, old bulky machines,

    Subpar computers and my prom.

Prom

We both are obviously concerned with each other's thoughts.

Our demeanor screams nervousness, am I sure I want to do this,

do, they like me, will this day go beyond today?

Is he watching me eat?

Does she like it when I do that?

My Nephew

My nephew just asked me for some white chocolate that I have in the fridge.

My nephew just did something wrong, so I must discipline him but not too harsh.

My nephew just ran through that tunnel at an amusement park because he saw a spider.

My nephew just came along with us to my friend's house to watch a movie and eat ice-cream.

My nephew just watched me sing in the choir at my church before going to the playground.

My nephew was there when my niece twisted her ankle at the playground, so sad.

My nephew enjoyed looking at the postcards in Chinatown and by the mall.

If You Should See

If you should see something in
my everyday work, my art
work, my pen to paper, (work)
then I would feel happy, I
would drink in oceans, I would
be appreciative to
work beside you somehow and
if you should see me looking
back at you just know that I
am the pen, tiny in your
palms, working with you to draw
it all.

Deadlock

A dusk shading,
meeting everything today,
gas and fire.

Stay

1.
The recipe,
stay ready,
across twelfth street.

2.
The walls tell me,
adobo,
Potatoes; love.

Impromptu

1.
You déjà vu,
coming loose,
replaying the clues.

2.
My umbrella,
lights so ruse,
keeping rain crystals.

3.
Rung sunlight young,
roaming hoot,
very impromptu.

World

Nobody wants world,
rather twirls with,
all our happiness.

Enshrine
for Alice Walker

When our bodies were before thought, we brought the layout
                        -flesh from divine parents
If only to play this game. Onslaught, hearts and minds
            organs and life, access and purpose,
                      enshrine.

Taking the Reigns

I want to address the irregularities,
the fact that you felt contained but
made every effort to live in the ethers
and define yourself by yourself and
say to yourself, your mind, I am enough.

For the ones who were less than perfect
according to their names and labels,
for the ones who made their own way,
own steps, own safe places, hooray
for doing things the way they were
meant to be done.

My Nephew Rose into a Silk moth (Part 1)

He had sex in my living room and excluded my devotion
to him. I dreaded him. His hobbies outweighed his responsibility,
and to me that was swordlike unjustifiable. I burned him into
my routine, losing no love.

He seemed to know my blueprint and I felt like God was
testing me.

So, I gave him calculators, pens, pencils, notebooks,
textbooks, you name it.
He quickly forgot my dedication, my expenses. My nephew
got rid of
his car (meaning I was now a chauffeur) a ridiculous move

making him the leader, answering his beck and call:
I was a gymnast, running, hydrating like fish: I gave him
slimy gas and lava (or lava cake). He enjoyed the gesture. I

surprised onlookers who viewed me as a snake with a once
chopped off tail. However, I decided to change.

My nephew knew nothing of carrying your own cross,
(weight),
overstayed his welcome and cared not to inquire about it.

So, I cleared everything I owned and left him to pick up after
Himself. I said a prayer for him and myself and I never
looked back.

My Nephew Rose into a Silk moth (Part 2)

I realized that maybe it was not his fault the cards that he was dealt

for this life, perhaps this was meant to be.

I let go of everything I thought had been done to me and I came back.

I couldn't forget the times when my nephew had come to my rescue,

And that story up until this continuation was one-sided.

There were times when he had to dig deep and be a rock for me,

be an all-encompassing box that said, "In these four corners you are safe. "

So now today, we go forth ready for blessings, new roads just going with

the flow. I don't claim to understand the cosmos, but all this really threw

me for a loop and now these new roads just go with the flow.

Need for Sugar

I am noticing my lack, my lack of the need for kisses, hugs, warm hello how was your day, oh and let me pick up the fallen jar of pickles for you.

I have always been rather independent and when I had romance and sugar so to speak, I appreciated it like the breeze of cold water on a hot humid day.

I am noticing my lack, my lack for sweet treats or just overly sugary things, you know the ones that get stuck in your teeth.

I have never been one to go to extremes so a twinkie was never on the menu. I have never been upset that I did not get my Twizzler or Skittles for the road.

So, I ask of you, what is the cost of your sugar because to some it might very well be amply worth it.

Spoiled Tasting Rain

The clouds spirit,
        simply true spirit
and spoiled tasting rain
        rinsing the air,
greenish vegetation and
        field shades that
spoke to me it's wisdom
        and arrows of love.
For once, I traded my home
        comforts for our clouds
Fast yet cold bones, partners alive
        and dead.
And when my child blind giving me
        rain, I say girl you are spoiled,
just so.

Magical Wall

My mother was the magical wall.
No-one questioned the wall when
the wall gave orders. No-one talked
over the wall because we were too
small and scared. The wall was just
cryptic to provide all our needs, we
never went hungry or felt any dry
stomachs. The wall cared for us
without showing too much affection.
The wall always contained its
emotion and rarely overflowed. This
wall was our only immediate
security or defense against anything
and often played both parental roles.
When I got older, I moved away, taking
marbles from this wall to keep for
memory's sake. Often when I talk about
my old wall, my associates tell me that
they too had such a wall, and I laugh to
myself.

Tiger Monsoon

Tiger plates are plenty
and awaits sharp like hunger,
meat never burnt and
adorned with veggies for the core.

Jayden Brown showing his teeth
burns in every chew.
A chew from these plates
beating in the tongue.

Chewing On Rocks

Growing up you realize that
your childhood friends, relatives
become more and more distant.
they call you less often, give less
blessings and celebrations. The
comfort of their voices is no
where to be seen.

I call for them sometimes in my
dreams and receive no answer.
In the past, I would think of some
memories in my mind and how I
missed them, and how our
Chemistry was epic. Today, I

understand that we have our
own lives and it's not necessary
to keep the same company.

The Breathless Tiger

Living life without happiness, let
him let go.

The public halls of his school, a
lop-sided goal.

The dusty papers rising and quick
sneezing has not gone.

That smell of spring galloping
our days ghosts.

Goodbye

I read a book,
                and my son thanked me.
I washed my car,
                and the shine said hello.
I welcomed a daughter,
                and my son thanked me.
I wept with the sun,
                and the shine said hello.
I laughed with the moon,
                and the moon shook my hand.
I said sorry to the sun,
                and the sun showered me with rage.
I said goodnight to the moon,
                and the moon smiled back.
I said goodnight to the sun,
                and all I heard was silence.

Juice through your Hands

You smell like tropical fruit and love to squeeze juice through your hands.

Water is your element from historical platoons of nature and things.

You have floated the bowls, cups and stomachs of our mothers, so I sing.

I sing with my heart and vibrations lift.

You are smart and well on its way to own,

a white rabbit ready to feast with you.

No drops are uneaten, you fill your mouth.

I am the future spoon.

You are pineapple, creamy in batches. I savor, I consume.

You are a mango left on the table.

I will feed you then show you the door.

Wisdom as I

I keep a lot of wisdom as I
enter every room. My white
strands of hair ease my middle-
age cries of joy which become,
the very color of my pale walls.
I learn things still that draw me.

How great is your parable,
so, to see futures and ancestors,
on my face, taking my eyes out,
morally with justice in the forefront.

Masterpieces

I hold onto masterpieces.
I hold onto masterpieces that renown my name.
I hold fast onto masterpieces for the wins.
You sold everything in the masterpiece,
or you sold your everything for the masterpiece.
I sold the masterpiece to my kids.
I sold the masterpiece and by doing so created more.
The masterpiece sold frees the essentials.
I sold no less than a masterpiece.
You sold sounds of your masterpiece.
The masterpiece sold made you jump for joy.
I guess, I sold you the first masterpiece.

Calculations

Thinking to calculate the black bars on a piano,
a surge of electricity through my computer goes,
around in my head but letting me own a simple
task. I calculate the dates, months, seasons,
temperatures, boy aren't you a hoot. I even
notice the rear view when considering small,
angles my boots have traveled. I do whatever,
floats my boat.

Printed by Libri Plureos GmbH in Hamburg, Germany